Black *girl* Interrupted

A Journey from Mental Illness to Recovery

Melinda R Hasbrouck
JD, MPH, Certified Peer Specialist

Global Book
Publishing

Black Girl Interrupted
Melinda R Hasbrouck

ISBN: 978-1-956193-44-2
Book Design & Publishing done by:
Global Book Publishing
www.globalbookpublishing.com

To Dad and Mom (Jeffery A. and Deborah Hasbrouck) – You gave us more than your best. I'm forever grateful to you.

To Natasha (Tasha) Suber Perry – My best friend, road dawg, and "sister," I cannot imagine life without you.

TABLE OF CONTENTS

Introduction

Are you tired of hiding your pain and pretending everything is okay when it hasn't been for a while? Do you know you need help but don't know what help looks like or where to begin? Are you afraid to move forward because you're scared of getting recovery wrong?

Maybe you or someone you know feels like I once did. I thought life was over when I started having problems with my mind—problems that were scary, overwhelming, and seemingly final. I was frustrated with life. I believed the door to life had closed on me. I thought death was the answer to my pain. I thought nothing would help, but I was wrong. Mental illness tried to break me, but by the grace of God, I became a survivor.

"Crisis has the capacity to birth your next move." That's what my Temple of Praise bishop, Glen A. Staples, said on July 20, 2022, in Washington, DC, as part of his thirty-first-anniversary message. This resonates with me because mental illness is, indeed, a crisis, and what you do with it defines your life. My journey from mental illness to recovery inspired me to write this book—and my book became my "next move."

Mental illness isn't the be-all and end-all I once believed it to be. I'm stronger for what I have survived. I'm deeper for what I've been through. I'm more compassionate for what I've experienced and seen. Mental illness is a part of my life; however, it doesn't define—at all—who I am.

I received a lot of help from some great folks along the way. When I mention being in recovery from serious mental illnesses, the room often goes silent, and heads spin to look at me. This is okay because I have their attention. Not too long after I share, others start nodding their heads in agreement, and people begin to say, "Me too." My desire is to encourage as many people as possible to have their "me too" moment.

Black Girl Interrupted combats myths and stigmas associated with mental health disorders.

"You can't talk about mental health—everyone will think you're crazy." Actually, many will feel relieved that someone is finally talking about the elephant in the room. The more you talk about your experience, the more you heal and the more others are influenced to seek help, which makes you a healer.

"You can't get help—it's too shameful." In reality, the more you focus on your mental health, the healthier you become. As a result, you'll ultimately find yourself equipped to deal with what life throws at you better than many people who don't have a serious mental illness.

"I'll never get better." Every day can be a struggle, and it still doesn't mean you have lost the battle. As time goes on, you can find a stable grip on your mental health and learn to manage the fluctuations in your life.

"Everyone has an opinion, and nothing fits me." You won't be tricked by one-size-fits-all solutions. Instead, you'll customize what mental health means to you. As such, you'll learn there are all kinds of treatments, activities, and much more to support your specific needs.

After you've finished reading this book, you'll be inspired to overcome the crisis of mental illness and embark on a journey to greatness. You'll see the day-to-day recovery process and be encouraged to press on. You'll believe that mental illness doesn't have to be the end of the road.

In Chapter One, you'll witness how I tried to escape from the hospital when others' good intentions went horribly wrong, and throughout *Black Girl Interrupted*, you'll learn about my recovery journey, learning myriad lessons along the way. Nothing means more than your mental health, so let's—without further ado—dive in!

ME AS A LITTLE GIRL

Something's Not Right in My Head

Fall 2009

"I need help, something's not right in my head," I said to the emergency department registration staff member.

"Have a seat and someone will be right with you."

"But I need help now. Something isn't right."

"Just have a seat and someone will be right with you."

I sat down and waited, feeling highly uncomfortable. My clinical support team had told me to go to the hospital if the offices were closed and I needed help. Here I was for the umpteenth time in the lobby of an emergency department. My head was spinning and making all kinds of distortions that to this day I cannot describe in detail. I knew I needed help, and I'd gone to the place where help was supposed to be. This time I'd gotten it wrong, though.

Thirty minutes went by. An hour went by, and I was all alone, mentally twisting in agony. I didn't have to be alone; my parents would have come. My best friend and others would have come, but by this time, I was isolated from everyone. I lived one mile from my parents and hadn't seen them in a year.

My former pastor walked by, and I got his attention. I told him what was going on and how no one had talked to me yet. He said he'd get right back to me—he was there to see a family member—but I didn't see him again.

Hmmph, I know how to get their attention, I thought. I took out my pill case and removed everything I thought would be fatal. I swallowed the remaining pills, not even considering that I could still be putting myself in serious danger. I wasn't trying to kill myself. I was trying to get help.

"Excuse me. I just wanted to let you know I swallowed all of my pills. You think someone can help me now?"

"You have a seat right there, honey, and someone will help you right away."

I bet they will, I thought.

Next came the routine I was used to by now. "Remove your clothes and put them in the clear plastic bag ..." I was allowed to use the bathroom to throw up the medicine I'd taken. Having actually tried to commit suicide before, I was surprised by the fact that they didn't even look to see what I had taken or if the pills came up. I was expecting the psychiatrist next and admission to the psych ward (a.k.a. mental health unit), but instead, two large men came inside with restraints in their hands.

"Get on the bed, ma'am."

"What are you about to do? I'm calm. I don't need restraints."

"Get on the bed, ma'am."

"Please don't do this. I've been raped. I'm not yelling or acting out or anything. Please, don't do this."

Then, they rushed me like we were playing football, picked me up in the air, and strapped me down to the bed by my wrists and ankles—far too tightly. By then, I was screaming foul and twisting, trying to get away. It felt worse than being raped because there were witnesses this time. Someone should have been helping me.

The psychiatrist finally made their entrance. I was sobbing, screaming, and squirming, asking anybody I saw to help me.

"Let's get her some Haldol."

"No, please. Ativan. I'm allergic to a lot of psych meds, and I've never had Haldol."

The doctor agreed and gave me a heavy dose of Ativan. He never asked what was wrong with me, what I was going through, or what happened to bring me to the hospital. I asked him to take off the restraints, and he says maybe in an hour. In response, I just lay in the bed, quietly sobbing. Eventually, after two hours, I had to pee and asked to go to the bathroom. The doctor approved the release of three restraints but kept my wrist cuffed to the bed. I was given a small bedpan and the use of one hand. As I went to the bathroom, the urine overflowed the pan and came crashing down, spilling all over me.

"Get back in the bed."

"Can I wash myself?" I pled.

"Get back in the bed now or all the restraints will be put back on."

Enough said. I got back in bed fast. Still, no one asked about what was going on with me. Next, I was transferred to another floor of the hospital. I didn't know and still don't know what kind of medical floor it was. I've been in and visited many psych wards, and this wasn't a psych ward.

"So, you tried to kill yourself."

"No, I didn't. I just ..."

"No, you tried to kill yourself. You took a lot of pills and tried to die."

"No, I was trying to ..."

"Enough, or I'll give you more medicine. If you call an adult to pick you up, I'll discharge you to them."

It was still the weekend, so my case worker wasn't available, and when I called the on-call system at my mental health agency, the case worker said he had too many people to see so he wouldn't be able to but would leave a note for my case worker. I finally decided to call a family member. I knew he'd understand and help me the one time I asked for help. He said he'd come to get me. Some time passed, and

I heard my mother's voice in the hallway. Instead of coming himself, he'd called my parents. If only I had known what this would mean...

I was at a place in therapy where I was exploring the anger surrounding my trauma. I was encouraged in my group therapy program, which focused on anxiety and trauma, to become angry about things that happened to me. Yet, I refused. I resisted.

"I'm good. I don't have a family like the other group members." I truly believed my family didn't have serious issues.

I'll never forget when one of the group therapists said, "Melinda, people who grew up in perfect families don't stick their finger down their throat to throw up after eating."

Dang. She had me there. Usually, I'm quick on my feet with snappy remarks, especially to emotionally distance myself from the person involved, the situation, or myself. So, I worked on being as angry as possible. And boy was I angry. I was *dangerously* angry because I was doing and saying things I normally wouldn't say or do, including how I honestly felt about all kinds of things. I heard the B-word mumbled more than one time throughout this period of rage. The homicidal thoughts I'd had since I was a kid were trying to come out fully. Becoming angry had released this identity of mine—a version of myself that wasn't taking anything from anyone. If you bumped into me, we had problems. If you said or did something, I would usually ignore you, all the while imagining your imminent death.

I had a dark, piercing look in my light brown eyes that conveyed to people, "Do not mess with me or you'll regret it." It was a dead look because that's how I felt. I didn't care about myself, anyone, or anything at this point in time. I sent letters, texts, and voice messages to those who had violently hurt me as a child or adult. Sometimes, I had to share in the art group sessions separate from the others because my "art" was causing others to "suffer." I would create art showcasing my feelings (at that time 100 percent anger without a filter) and share it with the group when I was allowed. Usually, I was compassionate and interested in what others shared. Not during this time, though. I would present, explaining what it represented if it wasn't clear. Unfortunately, members of the group would ask if my feelings included them as a group. Some thought they were safe from my rage. I told them it represented them too and why they'd all been included. My statements were honest, but they were mean and destructive—yet, I didn't care.

I don't remember how long this period lasted. I'm not sure who or what pulled me off the brink of this all-consuming anger, rage, darkness, hatred, etc. This is the only period in my life when I truly *hated*. I never use "hate" to describe anything or anyone because it's so definite—it's so 100 percent. I don't know how my fire had been extinguished, but eventually, it was. It left me with a vulnerable pain and hurt I had no way of protecting myself from, so I re-engaged with a slew of (maladaptive) coping mechanisms: bulimia, stealing, lying, sexual aggression, emotional distance, and suicidal thoughts, among other things.

Now, I found myself at the hospital turning my parents away. I don't know why I wasn't speaking to them at the time. But turning them away caused me to suffer greatly.

Back to the hospital. I asked everyone who came in or near my room what floor I was on. The nurses and the doctors said it was a medical floor, not the psych ward.

"So, I can leave, right?" I asked the nurse. "I can discharge myself against medical advice?" I hadn't even received any medical advice or treatment beyond Ativan, saline, and Pepcid.

"You can leave when the doctor discharges you."

This was bananas to me. I no longer knew what day or time it was, and I had no way of contacting anyone anymore. I decided to get out of there. It was time to escape.

I told the nurse that the IV put in near my neck was hurting and it needed to come out. My clear bag of clothes and purse were on the chair in my room, which was highly unusual, as I was being held for psychiatric reasons. The nurse removed the IV, and after waiting awhile, I dressed myself and walked out of the room to the elevators. I had to walk by the nurses' station, but that wasn't a problem because no one had interacted with me during my stay. I didn't even eat while I was there.

I made it to the elevator and was on my way to the lobby when I heard over the intercom, "Patient escape! Last seen ... Wearing ..."

Oh, snap, as my dad would say. I quickly pressed some random floor and left the elevator. It was like I was in a horror movie because I ended up on a floor that was clearly deserted. I couldn't lift the windows, and I wasn't going to go down the stairwell and bump into security. I got back into the elevator and headed to the basement. I knew the morgue was down there and figured it wasn't an area they'd check. I just had to keep my cool.

I was so close to the exit doors when two female police officers looked at me and asked for my name and identification. It was over. My escape had failed. Before I even had a chance to provide my name or a fictional one, they each grabbed me under one of my arms and dragged me to the elevator. When the elevator arrived, I was pushed into it and fell to the floor. We arrived back on the non-psych ward floor, and before I could get up, I was yanked by my arms and dragged out of the elevator. By this time, my case worker was standing there screaming at them to let me go—which meant Monday must have rolled around. All the while, I was thinking, *She's useless; the harm has been done.*

My stay was short-lived after this because someone had arrived to take me home. Before leaving, I had to agree to another shot of Ativan, though I wasn't in a state of distress. I was defeated, and my demeanor reflected my downturn. I wasn't talking anymore, and I'd accepted that they were going to do what they were going to do. My case worker was arguing to no avail, and eventually, we left.

She was scared to let me go home to an empty apartment—and my demeanor wasn't helping—so, we went to lunch first. But I'd been given an injection of Ativan, so I was slowly fading away and kept falling asleep. When I passed out on top of my burger face first, she said we could go.

The experience was so horrific that I became suicidal, and within twenty-four hours of being home, I called for help and went to another emergency department with my case worker.

Lessons Learned

- *Do **not** go to the hospital by yourself when you're in a psychiatric crisis. Even if someone has to meet you there, don't go alone. You're vulnerable, and too many are prone to going wrong, which means that harm can result despite what's intended. You need an advocate—a family member, friend, or someone from the community (e.g., a social worker).*
- *Never let anger interfere with your reality. If your anger is placing you in a position that's dangerous to your welfare, then anger is clearly defeating you. My parents would have advocated for me although they hadn't seen me in a while, but my anger wouldn't allow me to receive their help.*
- *Reacting in an extreme manner will get you an extreme reaction. I truly wasn't intending to kill myself. However, I can understand why the medical staff thought I was a danger to myself. Yet, I'm not excusing their behavior. I have a permanent back injury and suffered significant trauma, which took years to recover from.*

ME AS A CHILD

Has Anyone Seen My Self-Esteem?

"Girl," a grown man said to me—a grown woman. I was a little bit annoyed that I was being interrupted, given the fact that I was currently praising the Lord in church.

"Hi," I quickly replied.

"I'm going to get your number so we can talk."

"No."

I knew him to be sexually aggressive (yes, the world is in the church), and I just blurted out my response. But that "no" was a big deal for me.

Where had my self-esteem gone? I used to be able to say "no" without feeling like my stomach was tying itself in knots. These days, I didn't feel confident saying, "no," so I currently hid from people, fearing that they may ask me for something I didn't have the time or desire to do.

I had bipolar disorder long before an official diagnosis—a diagnosis that hadn't come in because the condition wasn't causing obvious dysfunction in my life. This hurt my self-esteem because I wasn't in touch with reality. I wasn't grounded, and things (like trauma) that should've affected me weren't being dealt with ... and this would later lead to my downfall. Trauma *will* find you. My current therapist had me read *The Body Keeps the Score: Brain, Mind, and Body in the Healing of Trauma* by Dr. Bessel van der Kolk. "The author uses recent scientific advances to show how trauma literally reshapes both your body and brain, compromising sufferers' capacities for pleasure, engagement, self-control, and trust." This is definitely worth a read.

Pre-mental illness, I was overconfident—with a wild degree of self-esteem 95 percent of the time. I was the kid and adult who welcomed peer pressure so I could tell you how idiotic you were and how stupid what you were suggesting was. I would also cite statistics and facts (honestly, some were made up) to convince you of my argument. Most walked away never to try again, and others eventually gave up. I was the kid and adult who had no fashion sense (I'm trying now) and didn't care, much to my best friend's anguish. Sorry, Tasha—lol. I believed in comfort and utility from a young age. I learned about bargain hunting for quality before I knew about styles and designs. I loved going with my mom and watching how amazing she was at being frugal—I thought we were rich because we never lacked for a thing. Don't mistake this with my mother's ability to say "no" firmly. We were spoiled, but we weren't spoiled rotten—some of us just *were* rotten.

I was the kid who asked for shoes from the *Blue Light Special* because I thought it was ridiculous to pay more than the lowest price possible for something that walked through spit and everything else on the ground. Also, my feet rapidly grew from about age seven, and my parents had to buy new shoes not much longer after I started wearing them. They stopped growing at size twelve in eighth grade (thanks, Dad, for flat, narrow, long feet ... without the height). Tasha warned me about what the kids were going to say to me at the bus stop and school. She shook her head in pity at the ridicule that was waiting for me. I was always ready, which apparently, I can also thank my dad for—namely, passing on his ability to make snide, snappy remarks that leave the audience laughing. (Sometimes, there's a delay before people understand that they've just been insulted, which only makes it funnier.)

I remember one of my favorite quips. A kid said for all to hear, "Menda, where did you get those creepers?" followed by fake laughter.

My answer: "Kmart or Sears Surplus."

Everyone proceeded to laugh.

Then, someone started singing the "cheap" sneakers' song: "Jeepers, creepers, where'd you get those sneakers?"

My rebuttal: "My shoes were $20. How much were yours?" Then, everyone (some clearly lying) start shouting out exorbitant prices (in the late '80s and '90s), that was about $80 on up. They thought they had made a point. Nope. My retort: "Well, that's dumb, seeing as how both of our shoes do the same thing and walk through the same stuff. And because mine are less, when I want to go somewhere or get something, I usually can because I'm not wasting my parents' money on stupid stuff." Silence ensued. Enough said.

Since we're talking about shoes and my self-esteem, I do have to point out one other favorite shoe battle. (There was a lot of focus on my shoes by other kids.) I went to an academy for middle school (public magnet school option) that had a uniform—and they were strict! We had to wear black dress shoes that most kids could get from Payless. Due to my flat feet and falling arches, I couldn't wear dress shoes because of the lack of support. No waivers at this school. My feet would have Charlie Horses almost every day, and they were awful. My doctor said I needed orthotics, which were these hard-plastic arches that fit great in tennis shoes because you'd replace the arch inserts with them. Not so much with dress shoes. So, my parents took me to the only place that could supply dress shoes in a size twelve and accommodate my arch insert. The results were black, old-people-looking shoes—like something a diabetic octogenarian would wear.

My best friend, Tasha—the poor thing—was horrified as usual when I showed her my new shoes. I was so happy and proud because my feet didn't hurt, and I wouldn't be violating the uniform code. I think Tasha was having a seizure because she kept shaking her head, saying, "No, Menda, no. Please, Menda, no." I wasn't worried, though. I liked them, and that was good enough for me.

Yet, so many people tried to attack me at school.

"What. Are. You. Wearing?!" asked one bully, and group laughter followed.

So, knowing that most of them were wearing Payless shoes or something similar, I went around the group and asked, "How much were your shoes?" Each person's answer was $10–$30 on average. "Well, mine were $80." Silence. Yes, I flipped the script, but I hope you see the parallels. If you don't, it's okay—you'll get there eventually.

I was also that kid who gave my parents a full report of the day immediately after school—at least the stuff I wanted them to know, which included *some* of my bad behavior. Before my dad got sick and was forced into early retirement, the stories were shared with my mom. By eighth grade, my dad was starting to hear them. Both were always proud and humored by my actions.

My mom was occasionally horrified, too. "Did you really say that?" That pattern continues to this day.

My self-esteem would continue to stay high throughout college and my first year of law school. Because it was so high, when something happened to me, I'd brush it off like it was an annoying fly.

My self-esteem would eventually crash when my mental health took a tumble. During the summer after my first successful year in law school, my middle brother was injured in a shooting and nearly died. A friend of his *did* die in the shooting. This shook our family to the core. It especially affected me in numerous ways. I thought if I'd only been a better sister to keep him away from the streets, this would have never happened. Now, I know myself to have been a great sister, but that's not what my mind convinced me of at this point in time.

Also devastating for me was the hidden trauma from childhood that fell off its shelf and busted wide open. I was remembering things that couldn't be true. To this day, I only have picture stills in my memory of things that happened during my youth. I was sexually and physically abused by someone close to our family for an unknown number of years. I don't blame anyone for not seeing the tragedy I was undergoing because I was presenting as the perfect kid with my self-esteem covering up the trauma unbeknownst to me. The child brain is amazingly adept at splitting its reality.

My dad's health declined at this time, and he had to be hospitalized for some serious issues, including his mental health. During this summer after law school, I would visit him every day and help with whatever I could. My dad didn't always remember who he was talking to while he was in the hospital. On one particular visit, the hit to my self-esteem felt like it had been delivered from a rocket launcher.

"Hey, baby girl. You come to visit me."

"Yes, Dad. How are you doing today?"

He would then tell me about his friends (the flies in the window) and his new stash of milk cartons. Then, he'd have me write down everything he wanted to buy and for whom. This was a normal visit until it wasn't. Also, my dad thought I was sixteen at this time when I was, in fact, twenty-five years old.

"Melinda, are you still going into the military?"

"That's the plan, Dad."

"Well, you know you'll need to lose weight."

My world imploded from that one brief exchange. My dad had been the only immediate family member who never commented on my weight. I was chubby. I was built like my dad but didn't have his height. My mom made comments, and my brothers were cruel about it, but my dad never had such an opinion. He'd always been impressed by how I'd work out and cook healthy meals for myself. I was devastated. From that point, my Teflon, non-stick, 100% self-esteem flatlined. Next, came the eating disorder.

Lessons Learned

- *All children need to be probed and questioned about whether they're safe at home. Not just the ones getting into trouble but the ones everyone loves to have in their class. This needs to be done in such a way that a child can trust the process. I didn't share with anyone because I thought my family would be destroyed, but I was internally begging for someone to see I was in trouble.*
- *There are signs that a child or young person may have a mental health disorder and need help. I was flying high, working two jobs while attending high school. I was attending extra school (visual and performing arts) and active in extracurricular activities. I didn't need much sleep, and my grades were stellar. The same thing in college but even more so. I worked five jobs, never missed class, and was active on and off campus. I was just considered "different." My fall would be severe and some of it could've been avoided if I had resources in place to help me. The "National Alliance on Mental Illness"*[1] *has good talking points and resources to help you figure out if something is going on with your loved ones or yourself.*

[1] *nami.org*

- *Talk about it. If I had talked to anyone about what my dad said to me, I doubt I'd have this book to write. Someone would have reminded me that my dad wasn't mentally well and that he loved his "baby girl."*

ME AS A TEEN

Want an Eating Disorder? I Did

"Well, you know you'll need to lose weight," said my dad.

Everything I had achieved up until this moment went out the window. This moment became the fracture in my life. This moment represents when I became the "black girl interrupted." My dad's innocent statement seemed to have been snarled, and he clamped down on me with his rabies-infected teeth. I died on the inside that day, and all I had left was my last piece of self-esteem telling me, "I'll show the world, I'm not ugly."

I had heard plenty of fat jokes by my twenties, and they generally didn't bother me. I grew up in a household with tall, thin people. It was my reality after a certain age: I was going to be chubby. I still did everything I wanted to do and was considered healthy.

One statement, though, and I was kaput—my mental health took a nosedive. It was a "Do not pass Go; go straight to jail" kind of fall. That's a reference to *Monopoly*, lest I lose you completely. It's not easy, but I'm going to further explore the fear, shock, and devastation I was experiencing then. By this time, I had graduated college and was a second-year law student. I knew what an eating disorder was in a general sense—something that makes you real skinny. Oh, they're so much more than this, though. It's like inviting the vampire into your home and future, and accidentally giving it the right to be with you everywhere you go once he crosses that door.

I became bulimic, bingeing on food and throwing it up on purpose. Yes, as a former law clerk and current law student, I used my advanced skills to diligently research the pros and cons of different eating disorders. I used clinical books, articles, and online chat rooms *promoting* eating disorders. Surprising?

Why not talk to my therapist, you might ask? I didn't have one at the time, and I didn't know how to "access" one. Access during this time was based on innocent ignorance. I accepted the internal voice in me that was yelling, "You're too fat, ugly, lazy, and pathetic!!!" The voice had gotten so loud this time that I accepted it was me, and the solution for the chaos and distress in my life was to be skinny.

As a reminder, soon before my commitment to bulimia, my middle brother, Tim, was injured in a shooting. It was devastating, as others were shot, and his best friend, Lil' Greg, died. For me, the trauma of not being able to keep my teenage brother out of a troubled lifestyle burdened me with guilt I couldn't process nor justify. I suffered silently because that's how I'd always suffered—I knew no other way. During this stage of silent grief, an older trauma fell off the shelf—something that I had packed away many years prior.

I started having these memories—picture stills and body memories—of something too horrific for me to believe true at the time. So, I kept pushing it away, and was so unsuccessful that I knew I needed a new way to "cope." The solution was inadvertently given to me by someone who was mentally sick at the time—someone who was so dear to me. Someone who had never thought I wasn't good enough. I knew my dad was sick and confused but that didn't mitigate the devastation I felt when he said I needed to lose weight so I could join the military.

I was so confident in my research and approach that I shared my plan with my godsister, Scarlet, and she was horrified and overwhelmed enough that she rightfully told her older sister, who was also my best friend, Tasha. I wasn't to be persuaded otherwise, though—as was usual. I could throw in some jokes, but we're going to stay right here with the "black girl" who saw no way out for her other than to eat humongous amounts of food and then stick her finger down her throat. I had many tricks of the "trade," but I won't share those because I don't want to support anyone going down this path, looking for an easy release of their pain.

Bingeing and purging food (bulimia) became my world. If I was experiencing anything uncomfortable, I'd go to food. I used food to squash all negative thoughts—anything hurtful or painful, guilt- or shame-ridden, along with traumatic memories trying to resurface ... and fear. If I couldn't sleep or wake up, I'd binge and purge. If I couldn't think straight, I'd binge and purge. If I imagined any discomfort, I'd binge and purge. I averaged about ten episodes a day. I should've been hospitalized because I was in a precarious situation causing harm to my immediate and future self. Yet, I was never able to access specialized treatment because I lacked insurance coverage, and the District of Columbia didn't have an eating disorder program that my public insurance would cover. My help was piecemeal at best.

For many years, I wouldn't accept that the traumatic memories haunting me were real. Instead, I thought I was sick—that only an awful person would imagine such horrible things. I was molested by someone close to my family as a child up to an unknown age, and I never said a word. I wanted to tell; I'd scream it in my head. I wanted someone to see my horror, but no one ever did. They only saw the success, the amazing wonder, the crowning achievement, etc.

I've been asked why I didn't say anything. It's not a fair question, but it doesn't bother me now. Part of my resiliency is that I can talk about things I couldn't handle back then, and it might help someone else. There's a simple answer to this question: I didn't know the words to tell anyone. Plus, no one asked me. It's sadly that simple.

Being honest with yourself, who pays attention to the golden kid, the overachiever, the one you want your child to be? Who sees that kid that gets all As when she wants to but is perfectly happy to buck the system and take Bs or Cs to irritate her teachers and others? The kid who's a voracious reader at home but only checks out the joke and cookbooks from the library because she knows the librarian is frustrated to no end. The kid who's in TAG (talented and gifted) but never passes the national tests because she doesn't try after finding out they're not designed for black kids. I have a million statements regarding "this kid" versus the "troubled kid." I don't blame anyone. I accept all the pain as the root of who I became and who I'm on my way to becoming. My purpose was being formed every time something unimaginable was being done to little Melinda. In 2022, this is how I currently think.

In 2002, I was dead and numb. I felt no attachment to myself. *Being skinny will fix everything, and then I'll be able to be the great person I'm destined to be*. As ridiculous as it may sound, I still occasionally believe it and I'm sure others who have suffered silently/loudly have believed it too. The difference now is that I do have a support system that includes professionals I can be honest with to help me do what I determine I want. Sometimes, that's helping me identify why I'm being triggered or engaging in bulimia—yes, even to this day.

The fantastic support I've had over the years includes people who understand how important autonomy is to me and that you lose me if you don't understand this vital component of our relationship. I'm still in communication with most of my individual therapists from the past—awesome, right?! One of my former therapists loved to remind me of one session when he was utilizing everything he had to convince me that I *did* want to stop bingeing and purging at the time. I had relapsed hard after a long time of not engaging in that self-destructive behavior. We laughed months later when he reenacted the conversation. His version was very funny because it captured exactly how I was feeling at that moment. Nothing he said or did was going to stop me. I was very firm that I did not care about any of the cons to continuing my engagement and I was dedicated to the bulimia—end of story.

I stay in recovery from bulimia as an active process every day. I still slip and manage to avoid full relapse by being honest with those who can help. My inner circle is well-defined, and its members love me very much. However, not all of them understand the mental health disorders I have and must deal with on a daily basis. I do love that they try, and their knowledge of mental health support and advocacy has grown phenomenally—for themselves, me, and their communities.

It's important that you seek support from the "right" people or programs, especially when you're vulnerable. I've learned that when I'm vulnerable, it's not the time to let my situation be a test or learning technique for others. It's time to take care of myself and not expose myself to comments made in love that can make things worse. I've reacted poorly in the past when I wanted something said or done but the person or program I was seeking help from wasn't the best source. Again, it's not a matter of judging myself or others; it's a growing pain that I thankfully survived.

Why in the world would someone research an eating disorder and then choose to engage in it after knowing the possible and likely negative health outcomes? You're missing the point if you don't consider that it's the fastest way to get skinny. I've included some pictures of me, along with the book cover, to show that unhealthy skinny does *not* look good on me. At my skinniest, you could see my bones, how tired I was, how disengaged I was, and how pale my skin had become. Even at my skinniest, though, I still wasn't skinny enough.

Every person trying to lose weight (eating disorder or not) has a number in mind. They might not say it out loud or voice the true number they desire, but they have one. Some people evolve to a healthier state of mind and set the goals as wellness goals instead of number goals. I applaud these people and sometimes I'm one of these people. Often, I'm not.

I never had a number goal until my direct descent into an eating disorder. I was very accepting of who I was—a chubby girl. I was active and healthy but had my dad's frame without his height. I was slender-average until around seven or eight years of age (pre-traumatic events). I was a kid that was usually running, jumping, swimming, hopping, climbing, dancing, and wrestling. I became a chubby girl after becoming immobile due to a leg fracture, and the weight never changed, although I maintained physical activity. I was the kid that won first place at Field Day for the hundred-meter dash. This girl could run! At a young age, however, I was beginning a descent into an undiagnosed eating disorder by sneaking and comforting myself with food. There were spurts of this, but I don't remember much more.

My first goal in 2002 was to lose a hundred pounds (I was 210 at the time), but publicly, I would say twenty-five. Eventually, my goal became to weigh zero pounds. What?! Yes, zero pounds was the goal! I won't take the time to discuss how ridiculous that sounds, but it's true. I lost eighty pounds in about three months because I was a subject matter expert in the process. My lowest weight was about 130 pounds, and that wasn't sufficient for me.

My weight goals were upended by a severe adverse reaction to an antipsychotic medication (and compounded by steroids) given to me in the emergency department. I gained all the weight back and more in fluid retention. Talk about distress? I became a hermit because I felt so ugly, and I was in pain from the fluid, too. I also couldn't take the immediate, unavoidable reactions of people who had seen me prior to the reaction. I concluded that every startled look meant I looked horrific. Self-confirming anything negative is a special skill set of my forever boyfriend, ED (eating disorder), the vampire you met at the beginning of this story.

Lessons Learned

- *You can become addicted to any behavior or habit, so choose wisely. I never thought that twenty years later, I would still be struggling with an eating disorder (ED). ED has kept me company for many years and patiently waits for an opportunity to enter my life any time I'm vulnerable.*
- *If you or anyone is researching ways to hurt yourself, help is needed immediately. Do not delay reaching out for support. If it's an eating disorder, a great resource is NEDA (National Eating Disorders Association).*[2]
- *The one statement from my dad wasn't my downfall. It was the straw that broke the camel's back. So much had happened up to that point. I was a powder keg ready to explode. If one comment from someone sends you over the edge, this is a clear sign that help is needed.*
- *Everything can't be one person's fault. Often, it's no fault of your own. My brother's shooting had nothing to do with me. I was vulnerable and came to believe that I'd had control over the situation and somehow failed to do my duty. In*

[2]*nationaleatingdisorders.org*

truth, I tried to help him, but he wasn't ready to receive my guidance yet. Question any belief you have that makes you think you had total control over something terrible.

ME IN MY 20S

The Very First Time

I wasn't stable anymore. I was back in Williamsburg, Virginia, for my second year in law school, and still doing the crazy commute to Rockville, Maryland, multiple days a week. My heart was in Maryland where my family lived, so I was all over the place. I had to return to school while my dad was still in the hospital, and I wasn't even sure what was wrong with him.

Fellow students were talking about what they did over the summer—where they clerked, vacationed, etc. It was the summer after 9/11, and the place I was supposed to clerk, the US Department of Justice, had never been able to process my background check. Clerks weren't a priority, understandably. Everyone was telling me how great I looked because of all the weight I lost. I told a couple of friends what happened (omitting the bulimia), but I didn't feel connected to coming back to school with all the torment in my life. I quickly became a recluse and started missing out on things I was involved in the first year.

My life consisted of going to class, going to my law school fellowship, going to work at the restaurant in Rockville, and as much as possible bingeing and purging. I stopped answering the phone, seeing people, and doing anything extracurricular. Every week, I was deteriorating, and there was nothing pulling me to safety. I faked every emotion. I faked being present when I was somewhere. I faked that everything was all right with me.

During my first semester of law school, I outlined classes and studied with two great folks. During my second semester, I reverted to my usual way of approaching school: attend class and study right before the exams. I had the same success, so I wasn't expecting anything different in the second year. Boy was I wrong!

Finals were coming up, so to set myself up for success, I took off from the restaurant and had nothing else on my calendar because we didn't have fellowship hours at the end of the semester. I planned to read the chapters again since I missed some classes when I couldn't get myself out of my apartment. Taking exams had never been a problem for me, so I really thought I'd be good. Day one of planned studying came and went without any studying. All I could do was binge and purge or sleep. Days 2–10 were the same as the first day.

I didn't know what to do. I was on day ten, the next day marked the start of the exams, and I hadn't studied any of the materials. The only thing I could think to do was visit a dean who had a kind demeanor and open-door policy. I met with her, and the conversation immediately broke me down in tears. I told her how the summer had gone—just the part about my brother and dad. I was too ashamed to mention the bulimia part. I told her how I couldn't study and the next day was the start of exams.

The dean asked if she could call the counseling center for me, and I said sure, not really knowing how that was going to help with anything. She did and I was told I could go over there immediately to meet with the director. I had never been anywhere near counseling, so I didn't know what to expect.

I walked into a very soft and engaging atmosphere. This was my very first time, and I was blessed when I compare how some of my other first times went when I engaged in new services. The receptionist handed me a clipboard with an intake form. Beyond the standard questions, I was asked about what I would later know to be the ACEs (Adverse Childhood Experiences). ACEs are traumatic events that occur before a child reaches the age of eighteen. Visit the Centers for Disease Control and Prevention's (CDC) website[3] for more information.

I looked at the ACE questions, stunned. I felt sick inside. I wanted to run out of the building, but I bravely started checking some of the boxes. This would be the first time I fully acknowledged the sexual and physical abuse that had happened to me. The intake form was also the first time I acknowledged I was having problems with an eating disorder. Moreover, the form made me face two unrealized facts: I was suicidal and homicidal. I patiently waited for it to be my turn, feeling completely nerve-wrecked and anxious but also intrigued, wondering how this place was going to help me take my exams.

---

[3]*cdc.gov/violenceprevention/aces/index.html*

Then, it was my turn to meet with my very first psychologist. After our hellos, I immediately start crying and didn't stop for hours. He kept extending the meeting an hour and offering me words of encouragement. He asked for permission to help me receive an extension on my exams and if I wanted to meet the next day. I would go on to meet with him multiple times throughout each week until the end of the semester—and then during the winter break. I barely talked at first. I just cried. I can't tell you how long I cried before I started talking about anything. I felt safe, though, filled with a profound sense of relief.

It would take years before I was no longer in crisis. When you've been suffering for decades, it takes time to work this stuff out. To God be the glory, and I thank Him for the fact that I was in safe hands throughout my first years of getting help. I was also connected to a psychiatrist to receive medicine to help with some of my symptoms of depression. I would later be diagnosed as having bipolar disorder; however, my first diagnoses were PTSD (posttraumatic stress disorder), major depression, generalized anxiety, bulimia, and suicidal and homicidal ideation.

I did finish my exams about a month later. I was told by our administrative dean that if I didn't finish all of them, then none of them would count. She didn't like me, and this was her way of trying to make me fail. She also felt insulted that I wouldn't tell her the specific reasons I needed to delay taking my exams. I was told I didn't have to tell her, so I refused.

The only negative aspect of seeking help was the secrecy surrounding my treatment. I was a law student, and to protect me, files would not be kept about my treatment. I would have to report the treatment on my bar exam application, but there wouldn't be any files others would have access to if requested.

A system of communication between my psychologist and the dean who referred me was also set up so if I needed to delay exams or assignments, the dean would be the only person told at the law school. This perplexed me, and I felt immediate shame about seeking help. I wish I had discussed this emotion, but I didn't know it had taken root.

Seeking therapy became the big secret I had in addition to all the other secrets I was maintaining. It would take ten years to feel strong enough to be open about my mental health disorders and the help I receive. I understand why such a system of secrecy was in place, but communities, families, and institutions are infected with stigma, and as a tragic result, people don't seek help. My purpose is to be loud and proud of my past circumstances so others don't avoid getting the help they need because of stigma.

I was encouraged to take the next semester off by my psychologist, but I refused. I had this notion that I needed to accomplish law school without disruption. It would've been better for me if I had taken the semester off, however, because my ultimate suicide attempt the next semester would force me to do so anyway.

Lessons Learned

- *Recovery takes time. I expected a quick turnaround, not a long-term investment. I remember thinking that if I gave therapy my all, everything would be good in six weeks. To my absolute horror, I was told to expect years. I started in 2002, and now I accept "recovery" to be an ongoing, continuous component of my life, and it must remain front and center for my mental health to be its best.*
- *Therapy is my best friend. It's hard work and not easy to challenge yourself on a regular basis, but I can't imagine life without therapy. Therapy is where I get to have the world just be about what I need and no one else. It's where my deepest thoughts, including my darkest and brightest, are discovered and nurtured. Long-term therapy isn't for everyone and not everyone needs it. However, I do believe that when major challenges come along, therapy is the best place a person can be—even if it's temporary.*
- *I was blessed to be linked to the counseling center when I finally couldn't pretend everything was okay any longer. I didn't know about accessing counseling for myself although it was right there and available. We need to do a better job of promoting counseling access and help. As*

a professor and advocate, I promote seeking help and specifically where to find the help based on the audience. The Substance Abuse and Mental Health Services Administration (SAMHSA) has a 24/7 national helpline (1-800-662-HELP [4357]), treatment referral service, and online treatment locator.[4]

- *Stigma is a dangerous thing. It prevents people from seeking help and/or keeps people living in the shadows. I want my life to represent proof that you can talk about mental health and still have a full life, including work and social opportunities.*
- *Environmental pleasantries aren't essential to a therapeutic setting. I've had my best sessions using video conferencing. The most important elements are a sense of safety, trustworthiness, and support.*

[4]*samhsa.gov/find-help/national-helpline*

ME IN MY 30S

I'll Die After Graduation

I was obsessed with suicide. Suicidal thoughts became part of my normal brain activity—always there reminding me I had an out. Only my psychologist knew I was suicidal. If I didn't talk about my mental health problems with anyone, I sure wasn't going to talk about being suicidal. I had an end date in mind: after I received my law school diploma. In my illness, I thought this would be acceptable to my parents—that they'd be proud I finished school. I didn't think of the people who would be hurt; I didn't have the capacity to consider anyone else's pain.

Being suicidal is like having a pan on simmer that's never turned off. It consumes you, and every moment you're closer to taking action towards dying. Every ding is compounded and felt hundreds of times worse than usual. It's hard to care about anything else or anyone else. There's a deep sadness that overcomes all aspects of your life.

Because I was planning to end things after graduation, my psychologist and I thought we had more time to work on my suicidality, but that wasn't the case at all. I was back to school the second semester of my second year, a walking shell of myself. I was frail and thin, only caring about bingeing and purging and attending therapy. I'd go to class and fail to take in anything being taught. I wasn't social with my cohort—I wasn't even saying hello anymore. Throughout the weekdays, I had therapy sessions or at least talked over the phone.

One nondescript day, I was tired of not being able to sleep, I was tired of the pain in my heart, I was tired of the thoughts telling me I was worthless and should die—I was tired of everything. In my naivety, I thought taking a whole bottle of medicine of any type would kill you immediately. I had a safety contract with my psychologist: I would not harm myself, including cutting without first talking to him. If I couldn't reach him, I would wait for him to call me back.

The safety contract had worked up to this point. I had willingly turned over numerous razors and other sharp implements to his custody. However, this time when I called and he didn't answer, I didn't wait. I was renting a room in Williamsburg, and I didn't want to make a mess for the others to have to see, so slashing my wrists was out.

I called. He didn't answer. I acted. As soon as I swallowed the whole bottle of Benadryl, I felt this immense guilt. The one person who had been there for me for over a year now was going to be so hurt by what I did. The contract was indeed working. I threw up the medicine and walked over to the campus police. I didn't want an ambulance showing up at the place I was living, and the campus police were within walking distance of where I was living.

The police staff was kind when I told them what I had done. They called an ambulance and sat with me until it showed up. I was immediately taken back to receive emergency services. I told them I threw up the medicine, but I still had to take a charcoal milkshake. If that sounds like it's gross, you're spot on. I couldn't keep it down and threw up all over the nurse. Lovely.

This hospital didn't have a psychiatric or mental health unit, so I was admitted to the general hospital. I had brought all the medicines that I was taking at the time, and they left them on a shelf in my room. A nurse served as a monitor in the doorway, and I remember thinking she was going to make me sick because she was coughing up a storm. She did, indeed, make me sick. All night, I thought about the medicine on the shelf and wanted to take it to finish what I had started.

I gave the hospital my parent's information, and my mom came down from Maryland the next day so I could be discharged to her. No one at the hospital had talked to me about what happened, and my mom didn't know what to say on the ride back to Maryland. I surely didn't know what to say, so I said, "I didn't want to talk about it." My mom respected this, but I was really yearning to talk about it all. I found myself back in the same place I'd been trapped as a little girl, being hurt, wishing I could talk to my mom to get help but not having the words to start.

My old bedroom was available, so I lodged there when we returned to the family house. Unbeknownst to my parents, this was the room where I was abused. It all became too much for me, and I knew I was going to complete suicide if I didn't get out of there. I asked my mom to take me to the hospital where I knew there to be a psychiatric unit and admitted myself for safety.

I had been to the hospital many times, particularly this one. They placed me in a shared room. Yet, I don't think it's the best practice to implement double occupancy in a psych ward. This admission I was feeling defeated and hostile. My suicidal and homicidal ideation was ramped up—I wasn't being my usual polite self. I was put in a room in the middle of the night and came close to harming my roommate.

Imagine you being at your worst and being placed in a room with a roommate who's snoring louder than anything you've ever heard in your life. On top of this, she's half-dressed and her bare bottom is exposed for you to just stare at in horror as she passes gas every few minutes. This was my reality. I took out my art book and drew the scene of the murder I was about to commit. I placed the drawing on her bed and went over to my bed to gather some pillows. As I was walking to her bed with the pillows to suffocate her, a nurse opened the door.

"Oh dear," the nurse said to me. "How on earth are you expected to sleep with all that noise?"

I said nothing, standing there, holding the pillows, waiting for her to leave.

"Let's get you moved to another room—one by yourself." The nurse saved two lives that night.

It was time and work devoted to healing that would end the noise of suicidal and homicidal thoughts. After ten or so years of being ravaged by thoughts, I found myself in a blissful silence one day. It wasn't luck; it was a blessing. Having achieved this silence, I know it's possible to recover from a suicidal or homicidal frame of mind. I'll still have thoughts of suicide, but they're manageable—simple signs that I'm hurting, which I address in therapy. I know others who have progressed out of ideation too, and they credit healing work, which includes a plethora of methods based on what was best for them.

Lessons Learned

- *I was so lonely during my suicidal years. It wasn't something you could chit-chat about. I didn't know about free support groups in the community like NAMI DC (National Alliance on Mental Illness, DC Chapter).*[5] *I would later learn about many programs and other fantastic services. Being resourceful would become my survival tool.*
- *It's important to have a safety contract and crisis plan. These don't need to be long—just direct. I've included an example of one you can customize to satisfy your needs.*
- *If someone is suicidal, they usually* **do** *want to talk. Talking to someone about suicide can mean everything. This has been my experience—and that of countless others. So many have asked me if they think talking to a suicidal loved one about wanting to harm themselves will cause that loved one to commit suicide. Indeed not. The person who is suicidal no longer feels seen, and they're hurting badly. Paying attention to them will help them.*

---

[5] *namidc.org*

- *Being suicidal is a chronic condition. It's always there in the background. Flareups happen and you feel more suicidal than other times. A suicide attempt is an acute condition. It happens suddenly, and it very often fails to go as planned. I couldn't handle what was going on anymore, and I suddenly tried to commit suicide. This nature makes being suicidal a highly dangerous condition. Don't delay in getting help for yourself or a loved one if they're expressing suicidal and/or homicidal thoughts. 988 has been designated as the new three-digit dialing code that will route callers to the National Suicide Prevention Lifeline.*
- *Never take someone's expression of wanting to hurt themselves or others lightly. Please don't ever dismiss it. You may not be the best person to help them, but you can guide them to others who will. You don't want to become their crisis counselor either. It's important to maintain boundaries and let professionals step in to help when appropriate.*

Mental Health America (MHA) has made a crisis plan available to the community free of charge.

HINGS TO LOOK OUT FOR

ggers are people, places, words, or situations that :rease negative feelings. They can make it difficult cope with mental health symptoms. When you're :ll, it can be helpful to work on exposing yourself to ggers so that negative experiences are lessened ıen you're stressed. For example, if going to the ɔcery store or crossing bridges is scary – take small :ps to expose yourself to these situations. There are me triggers, like yelling, or abusive relationships ɪt you might consider avoiding all together. :ntify some triggers that you can work through. ıd identify if there are triggers that you should ɔid.

TRIGGERS

____
____
____
____
____
____
____

rly warning signs are personal changes in oughts or behaviors that signal that things are tting worse. The sooner you intervene when these ȷns occur, the better. Use the lines below to think out your early warning signs. Some examples ight include: withdrawing for more than two days, :ling so agitated you haven't slept for three or ɔre days, or finding it difficult to get out of bed. hen these signs occur, it's helpful to list out your xt steps for seeking help. This might include lling your treatment provider, or calling your ıergency contact.

Y EARLY WARNING SIGNS

____
____
____
____
____
____

EPS TO INTERVENE

____
____
____
____
____

ACTIONS TO TAKE

Stress can creep up on you when it seems like y have so much to get done and not enough time do it. Or sometimes when symptoms of ment illness come back, normal every day activiti become stressful. When stress comes, it often affe sleep. Use the lines below to identify steps you c take to reduce stress. You can use the list below get started.

THINGS THAT MAKE ME FEEL BETTER

____
____
____
____
____
____
____
____
____
____
____
____
____
____
____
____
____
____

1. Make a routine.
2. Stand up and stretch.
3. Take 4 slow, deep breaths.
4. Do a puzzle or color.
5. Talk to someone who is a good listener.
6. Give yourself a pep talk ("I can do this.")
7. Close your eyes and listen to sounds around you
8. Look at animal pictures. Who doesn't like a pupp
9. Watch a funny video.
10. Take a brisk walk.
11. Read a magazine.
12. Watch the sunrise or sunset.
13. Massage your temples.
14. Do a good deed or random act of kindness.
15. Listen to music.

MHA B4Stage
Mental Health America

ME IN MY 40S

A Semester Off

Because I went to the campus police station for help with the suicide attempt, the law school medically withdrew me for the semester. I was never supposed to come back. No one knows what to do with a student who attempts to kill herself. There were quite a few completed suicides at William & Mary, and the school didn't take the threat of another one lightly.

I found myself back at home feeling like a failure—a law school failure and a suicide failure. I was still in contact with my psychologist, so I didn't feel like I had been kicked out of the environment completely. He knew I wanted to complete school, which meant I wanted to come back to school after the summer. This meant I had a lot of work to do while I was back home. Giving up wasn't an option.

The strangest thing to me is how hard I fought to live while being suicidal. I had to learn to navigate a broken public health system while I was fragile, vulnerable, and in crisis. I had changed my residency to the District of Columbia a couple of years before my suicide attempt, so I started seeking local services. I went to a community health center to get a primary care doctor. They took insurance and used a sliding scale to zero for those who couldn't afford to pay. I had just aged out of military-dependent insurance and had zero income. I had a checklist of what I had to have in place for William & Mary to consider my request to come back after the suicide attempt.

I had been engaging in bulimia for two years before the suicide attempt and had lost over ninety pounds. I was thin and frail. I was used to seeing the medical doctor for a weigh-in and my psychologist multiple times a week while I was attending law school in Williamsburg, Virginia. There were so many things going on with me regarding safety that focusing on my trauma history and eating disorder had never been a priority. It was a "we'll get to that when we can" type of situation. The focus was rightfully "keeping Melinda alive."

Part of my requirements was to check in with a primary care provider and a psychiatrist. I was blessed to have access to my Williamsburg-based psychologist via telephone. I had been in therapy for over a year but still couldn't bring myself to talk about the trauma I had experienced as a child. Most of our sessions focused on my safety, as I was severely suicidal and finding new ways to hurt myself on a regular basis.

Bulimia was my primary coping strategy, and I was happy with the results. Now, I was being told I couldn't return to law school unless I had stopped engaging in bulimia for a specified amount of time. I had to stop cold turkey. For two years, I was bingeing and purging on average ten times a day, and now I would have to just stop.

That didn't go so well.

"Melinda, black people don't get eating disorders. I don't know how to help you," said my new primary care doctor. "Black women are supposed to be curvy." At least she was honest. I knew from her statement this was going to be one tough summer.

My primary care physician referred me to the in-house psychiatrist, who wasn't like the one I had in Williamsburg. He was curt, aggressive, and hostile—to put it politely. I was told that under no circumstances would I need to talk to him about my childhood trauma, but he wouldn't respect my decision. He would make us have biweekly sessions in cramped rooms and occasionally at the men's shelter where he worked. Mind you, I was deeply traumatized at the time. I was nervous, on-edge, and ready to run if a penny dropped on the floor. My flight-or-fight instincts were ramped up to 300 percent.

This psychiatrist wanted to hold my hand, made me look him in the eyes when he talked, and expected full compliance with whatever he said. I didn't know enough yet to get the heck out of his environment, so I suffered through every injustice. He was also putting me on all types of medications and outright dismissed the trauma I had experienced as a child as normal. There's no nicer way to put it than to say this man was a quack.

Dr. Quack prescribed me so many medications, I couldn't keep up. One medicine made me pass out for a literal week on my parents' couch. I would come to find out that I'm very sensitive to psychiatric medicines and usually can't come near the average starting dose. I wasn't sure what he was trying to medicate because we never talked about symptoms other than bulimia.

I feared Dr. Quack because he had the power to keep me out of school, so I'd go along with whatever he told me to do. He insisted I stop bingeing and purging, so I stopped and reported that I stopped. I had no other way of coping yet, so I switched to a full-on restriction of food to keep me away from bulimia. I'd make it so far and then relapse with a binge and purge episode. I felt guilty that Dr. Quack thought I was having a smooth ride, so I told him one day at a meeting about the relapses.

"Um, I know I told you I wasn't engaging in bulimia anymore, but that's not completely true. I've had slipups along the way."

"What?!" Dr. Quack said angrily.

"I tried really hard but couldn't do it. I'm sorry for leading you on."

Dr. Quack suddenly stood up in my face and pointed his finger right at me and said, "You're a liar by omission and commission. Get out of my office!"

As you could imagine, I was horrified. I ran out of his office, seeing my law school career diminish in thin air and thinking of how horrible of a person

I was. I had taken the subway to see him, so I ran off, intending to jump in front of a train. The DC Metro staff is highly trained to intervene when they see people in distress. A man in uniform suddenly appeared and asked me if I was okay. I wasn't, but his stopping me paused my distress for long enough for me to realize I needed to get to a phone and call my psychologist. This was in 2004, so it wasn't as simple as making a cellular call.

I took the metro back to my primary care provider's office and asked the security officer if I could use the phone to make a long-distance phone call. I was clearly upset, so he took me to a room to allow me some privacy and the use the telephone. When I reached my psychologist and told him what happened, he said, "Melinda, you never have to go back to him again. Never. We'll figure something out." I never had to see Dr. Quack again, and the times his path has crossed mine in our small city, I've turned the other way before he could see me.

My next move would be to enter a core service agency, a public mental health provider. I had taken family to an agency to drop them off, so I decided to try it out for myself. The place was utilitarian—not at all like my first counseling visit, but it was clean and efficient. I walked in, not knowing if I'd be able to get any help, and left with a new psychiatrist, a case manager, and a completed public health insurance application. The agency would play a vital role in helping me survive crises, get back on my feet, receive Social Security Disability Insurance (SSDI) benefits, and learn about "recovery."

I was able to return to school for the fall semester, but because I hadn't really had the time and support during the summer, it was another turbulent semester. I had to decide whether to invest in my health by taking another semester off or accept the six-figure job offer post law school. I believed my psychologist that I might make it a year before collapsing if I didn't make one of the hardest choices in my life. So, I took one more semester off and finished my last semester off-campus. I successfully graduated from law school, but it would take over a decade for me to be proud of myself for the accomplishment and recover from turning down the job offer.

During my second semester off, utilizing my advanced research skills, I found an outpatient program, a day center for trauma and dissociative disorders at a local psychiatric hospital. I self-referred to their services in 2005 and greatly benefitted from their group-style clinical treatment. On my first day, I was asked what I was doing tomorrow and the days that followed. I wasn't doing anything but therapy, so I was told to come five days a week and treat it like my full-time job. I was experiencing severe depression at the time, so that sounded like a good idea. After some time, I attended the program 2–3 days a week for months. I gave it my all, and because of this, I made leaps and bounds in trauma recovery and began to move on from bulimia. I was also blessed to meet my current therapist at the program. He would become my private therapist almost fifteen years later.

Lessons Learned

- *The nicest people sometimes can't help you. My new primary care physician didn't know how to treat eating disorders and was honest about it. Instead of being upset, I had to reassess my plan of action. I needed her to take my vitals and check in with me, so she worked out fine.*
- *Never force a therapeutic relationship. I didn't know any better and thought I had to take what was being offered to me. I still only had one knowledgeable source of support at that time, and he was in a different state. This is another reason we can't let stigma grow its dirty little roots. I didn't know anyone who was talking about their experiences to gather advice from and was left on my own to figure out vital pieces of the puzzle.*
- *When you're in extreme duress, something to stabilize you is needed immediately. For me, it was the kindness of the Metro staffer, but other times it's been something as simple as splashing cold water on my face or telling myself, "Stop, stop, stop, stop."*
- *Heroes are all around us. The Washington Metropolitan Area Transit Authority has seen its share of suicides by train or third rail. Thus,*

they became their own crisis intervention squad by knowing signs of distress. I remain grateful to the angel that helped me the day I was going to jump. I never had a chance to thank him. I'm sure there are many transit systems that have taken these initiatives, and if they haven't, it's never too late to start.

- *Don't rush your recovery. You owe it to yourself not to skip through the pain of getting to the other side. You may want to throw in the towel at first, but after a while, you'll know you've made the most important investment you ever could: putting yourself first and getting your needs met.*

JEFFERY A & DEBORAH HASBROUCK
DAD & MOM

Living in My Ride

I slowly moved into my truck as my mental health declined. After a year and a half of ravaging depression, I started having manic episodes. Merriam-Webster defines *mania* well: “excitement manifested by mental and physical hyperactivity, disorganization of behavior, and elevation of mood.” While I was taking the semester off, I returned to a restaurant I used to work at during my undergrad studies.

One day, a co-worker asked me for a ride home and I told her I wasn’t sure if I had enough room. She looked at me strangely, knowing I had a seven-passenger vehicle (Montero, SUV) and no one else riding with me. I’m known to keep a junky vehicle, but usually, I just push/throw/shove stuff aside to make room for people. This time, I really didn't have space due to the regular-sized ironing board taking up a lot of space among other household items, work uniforms, books, and clothes. Ironically, there wasn't an iron in my truck to accompany the ironing board. By this time, I'd been living in my truck for a while.

Before you feel pity and think I was homeless, that wasn't the situation at all. I was paying rent to share a townhome with my best friends in Silver Spring, Maryland, and renting a room in a home in Williamsburg, Virginia. I was back to attending classes. I had other options, including my family home in Capitol Heights, Maryland, and many friends who offered me a space to live after they found out I was living in my truck. I also didn't need to work and wasn't supposed to work more than ten hours a week as a general law school rule. So, the best option I had was to not live in two areas so far apart while I was in law school, but I wasn't rational. I didn't one day make the decision to move into my truck, it happened slowly and "logically" (according to me and my therapy team).

It started while I was in a manic state of mind, working 90–100 hours per week in Rockville, Maryland, while attending law school in

Williamsburg, Virginia, which was about 180 miles away. One night after work, I drove home to Silver Spring (not far from my workplace) and fell asleep after I parked. My bestie, Tasha, eventually realized I was outside and woke me up, telling me to come in. This happened a few times, and one night I said I would be in but never got out. That's how it started. I would come home and sleep outside. I'd sometimes go in to wash clothes and take care of other personal things, but I started to sleep in my truck. Eventually, I started to sleep in parking lots near my place of employment and sometimes on a bench inside the restaurant.

People already knew I was weird. I was called Crazy Menda—not in a derogatory or mean way. I've always been very different. So, I understand some people just taking my new residence as another element of my weirdness. What they and I didn't know at the time was that I was rapidly declining in my mental health. My mania wasn't yet controlled well, and symptoms of PTSD (posttraumatic stress disorder) were running rampant.

I started to like living in my truck and accepted it was the safest place to live while others tried to convince me of the dangers of living outside in a vehicle that had no tint or alarm. I was convinced they were wrong, and my truck was the safest because of one indisputable fact: I had never been sexually or physically assaulted, abused, raped, etc. in my truck, but that had happened to me many times in "homes" as a child and adult by people close to my family and friends, medical staff, and a date. Trying to sway me at that time with "hard facts" was a lost cause. My logic was irrefutable. My truck was my pal—I needed nothing and no one else.

I slept in places that were well-lit. I had my pillows, pajamas, and a comforter. I disappeared under my covers, and you would never know someone was in the truck. Oh, except for the many people walking by or sitting next to me in their vehicles I startled when I'd pop up suddenly. Usually, I'd pop up to use the bathroom urgently. This also meant I had to sleep near places that had restrooms, although I did pee outside numerous times. I had no shame and still don't about using the bathroom outside. My saying at the time was, "I can squat like sasquatch."

Once, in an enlightened moment, I thought I should use incontinence underwear (pee protection) because I was tired of nearly peeing on myself when the urge hit me. Yes, I did. Tried it once and never again. I wore them, and I had the urge to pee. When I pee, I pee. So, the diaper overflowed. Nastiness! Shaking my head at the thought. I had to clean and air my ride out after that experience.

Because I was sleeping in the vehicle, I started falling asleep behind the wheel while I was driving. I was dumbfounded in a therapy session, discussing my inability to stay awake for more than about five minutes no matter how much sleep I was getting. My psychologist at the time explained that my body thought it was time to sleep when I was in the vehicle. This started happening when I was sleeping in the driver's seat because I had run out of room in my truck to sit anywhere else.

When I first started sleeping in my truck, I would sleep in the middle like a bed. As my mental health continued to decline, I kept bringing stuff in (the details are hazy). I still would throw something over me to sleep so people couldn't see me in the vehicle. But now sleeping in the driver's seat was confusing to my already disturbed mind. I would fall asleep while driving, realize it, and try to exit or pull over, falling asleep along the way. I hit curbs and side rails and even crashed into the Jersey wall on the beltway, only stopped by water barrels and the grace of God.

I never hit anyone or anyone's car, so don't try to investigate hit and runs. The Holy Spirit was working overtime. I'd wake up in neighborhoods, not knowing where I was or how I got there. Later, I discovered some of these neighborhoods, and it was always humorous to say, "I slept there and there and there" and see the expressions on people's faces as they began to process though they weren't ready to ask. Sometimes, I'd have to drive around to look at license plates and signs to know what state or city I was in.

Because I was so honest with my psychologist and psychiatrist, they decided at a certain point—me crashing into the Jersey wall—that enough was enough. They both had earned my trust, and I felt safe around them. I think I gave my psychologist gray hair during this period, which I really feel bad about—oh, the stress I caused him! I was worried that my license would be taken away from me, but it never rose to that level. My psychiatrist at the time threatened me with an option: come in every day to my community health center to get my medicine or stop sleeping in my truck.

My doctor and psychologist knew enough about me to know autonomy was important to me—and it still is. Threaten to take away my freedom or try? It's on and poppin'. I'll react so fast; your neck will snap. Sometimes, my reaction can be scary to me *and* the person on the receiving end. It would've been nice to have more time to work out the issues keeping me in the truck, but I understand my safety was an issue. So, I stopped living in my truck after six months and moved in with a Gambian family—friends of mine. That lasted for another six months before a big lie was told about me and it no longer felt safe to stay there.

Lessons Learned

- *Feeling "safe" is at the core of my trauma-related issues. Whether I feel safe or not tends to determine which version of Melinda shows up. I'm a chameleon until I know the lay of the land.*
- *My safety has been affected so many times that trusting a person won't hurt me is hard to accept. However, if I don't trust anybody, I don't make the connections with each other we all need to function in this world.*
- *Autonomy is important to everyone, no matter their age. The more a person has power over the things that directly affect them, the more they'll be receptive to those things. Yanking my license probably would've thrown me further off course, and I would've lost trust and my sense of safety.*
- *Sometimes, we can't wait for a person to get it together. My therapist and psychiatrist knew the danger I was putting myself and others in and had to intervene. The intervention is going to be different and should be different depending on the individual. The worst thing that could happen is for a person to lose all trust and quit the "system of care." It would've been nice to have*

the opportunity to work the vehicle safety issue out, but the more I drove, the more dangerous I became.

THE HASBROUCKS

Baking for Survival

During the first four years of mental illness in my mid-twenties, I was always in a state of crisis. I'd move from one crisis to the next, and they all had a theme: trauma history, suicidal thoughts, and/or bulimia. I was initially a client of the trauma team at a community mental health agency. Every appointment during the first years focused on crisis prevention, survival, or clean-up.

I was living in a one-bedroom apartment provided by the agency, and after three years there, the building was going to be renovated and I needed to move to another location. The housing we found for me was on another team: the recovery team. This was a foreign term to me at this point. I was curious what they meant by "recovery." I thought life was over for me and I had no future to look forward to given my circumstances.

I'd been dealing with mental illness long enough to accept this was it for me. I'd be a glorified volunteer and the person who was always there to help family and friends because I had nothing else to do but jump from crisis to crisis. My life was full, but it wasn't close to the life I had planned on living. I knew there was more, but I wasn't there yet and I couldn't see how I'd get there.

The word *recovery* was given to me at the age of thirty-three, and I pounced on it. I started looking for new ways to recover from my circumstances. I understood recovery to be a process, as it pertains to mental health. Usually, if you break a leg, with time, patience, and maybe rehabilitation, you recover from the injury. Mental health disorders require recovery to be a discipline like how maintaining nutrition, weight, and sugar levels is the goal for a person with diabetes.

One serious problem I needed to recover from was hooking up with guys because they made me feel pretty.

"Can I have an STD test?" I asked my primary care physician.

"Oh no, Melinda. Not again" she said. "Are you still getting help with this?"

"Yes, I'm still in therapy and stuff."

I was out of control. I felt like I wasn't making decisions anymore. I was just reacting to emotions. A guy would say I was cute and then I'd find myself having sex with him, usually unprotected. Nothing in therapy was working to keep me away from these repetitious scenes. Basically, I was a sex worker who wasn't getting paid for her sex work. I didn't know what to do, but I was frustrated with the way I was living. I was playing out my trauma history and picking up new traumas in the process.

I can only thank God for keeping me STD-free and for the intervention that would keep me celibate for years and off the streets. Baking became my survival tool.

When I was a kid, our house burned down, and because of this, I won't leave certain appliances on when I'm not home. Our house didn't burn down because one was left on, but it's a risk I still refuse to take. So, I knew that if I were to bake a cake, I wouldn't step out while it was in the oven.

Because I was a professional baker, it didn't take long for me to whip up a cake, so one cake wasn't going to cut it. To keep myself in my apartment, I would need to bake for hours when I'd get the urge to roam the streets. This intervention worked. The only problem I'd run into was having multiple cakes, pies, cookies, etc. to get rid of multiple days of the week. Although I was still quite bulimic, I didn't indulge in the goods because this was meant to be a healthy coping mechanism for me. The public mental health agency I received services at had no problem helping out in this regard. My peers were quite happy to eat the goods.

Baking is part of my core reflex. I've been baking since I was a young kid in elementary school. I wanted to cook by putting a chair next to the stove and standing on it. I selected recipe books from the library at school. The librarian always tried to convince me to check out more stimulating books than jokes and cooking. Why? I was so advanced in reading that I was in a group of classmates that had our own special reading time away from our peers.

In time, I ran out of joke books. It's no longer funny when you know the answer to every punchline, and everyone else who I victimized with my corny, child-appropriate jokes was tired of me and knew the answers, too. So, cooking sounded like a good idea. Chair at the stove? "Um, no," my mom said firmly. Never being one to easily give in or up, I asked about baking since I could pull down the oven door and I was big enough to not accidentally become a victim of the Gingerbread Hag (the witch from *Hansel and Gretel*). I'm sure my mom taught me about safety and how to watch the oven, but I don't remember and I'm not completely confident that she did.

I outbaked my mom, surpassing her skills by my third attempted recipe. Not to say we didn't enjoy the seven or eight recipes she could make (or *chose* to make; she wasn't really trying if you ask me). She made Jell-O, banana pudding, brownies, pineapple upside-down cake, coconut cake, and yellow cake with chocolate frosting. Honestly, I never saw her making anything else. My mom isn't a measurer either, which drove me insane. How do you learn from someone who pours and never has a consistent outcome? She'd often say, "How do your brownies come out so perfect?"

I snidely remarked (a safe distance away, so as not to be disrespectful), "I follow the directions and measure." Lots of people ask me if I learned how to cook/bake from my mom. Nope.

I loved making food and watching people enjoy consuming it. I hardly ate anything I baked or cooked as a young kid for two reasons. I didn't have a sweet tooth, so the desserts weren't appealing after a quality-testing bite. The food I was cooking when I was old enough to use the stove looked scary to me, especially since most of it was some experiment from a book I read. One such incident involved me cooking "gumbo." Anyone who knows how to cook gumbo is going to drop dead from shock when they read this passage. I was hooked on this one book. It was a tween book about a girl who isn't the typical "princess," which I always related to. I'm my dad's princess, but I also was raised by both of my parents, so I know how to build a house, wire and setup all technology, bring the bacon home, and cook a five-course meal. Hey, not to say that I don't want a male companion in life to share my future with, but I don't need him to complete me.

So, one passage of the book was about the group getting stuck during their camping trip. I'm doing this from memory, so I'm sure I'm getting most of the details wrong. Basically, they were stranded near a cave and only had a cooler of random food to eat. They tossed it all in a pot (hot dogs, cheese, beans, vegetables, fruit, etc.) and boiled it. They called it gumbo I think, and everyone ate so they wouldn't starve to death. I read this book so many times that the cover literally fell off and some of the print was smudged. I usually don't read books twice and I'm practically a speed reader. I loved this book because it literally made me laugh out loud over and over.

Sometimes, I would cook for the younger kids in the family when my parents weren't home. I was older now and knew what to do in case of fire in the kitchen—run! Just kidding. I knew to smother it. I was inspired by this gumbo when I couldn't find something to put together in the kitchen for the kids. So, I started throwing everything into this stockpot: frozen and canned vegetables, elbow macaroni, canned soup, bologna, cheese, chips, and something that was red. It bubbled like a witch's brew. Bright blood-red "gumbo." I gathered the children together—likely Shaniqua, Timotheus, John Face, Nincompoop, and Konnichiwa. No, those aren't their real names, but that's what I called them and still do occasionally (Chawndra, Tim, Johnathan, Nikki, and Kenny).

We played restaurant. I was the hostess, waitress, and cook. I seated them at the table and placed reusable plastic plates, cups, and mismatched silverware (because we'd often accidentally throw away some of it) around the table. I grew up on child-safe dishes and still am a little uncomfortable eating on glass plates at home. Because we all were kids, we acted out things we'd seen on television or at the movies. They were mean patrons who banged their silverware while yelling, "Feed us! We want food!" I'm every kid's fantasy and that's why even to this day, kids aged two and up flock to me because I'm willing to treat them as the intellectual, creative masterminds they have already become.

I thought the kids wouldn't eat the blood-red gumbo because I sure as heck wasn't eating it. They loved it, though, and asked for seconds and thirds. I never saved my parents any food to eat. My mom was nice about my creative cooking skills, always claiming not to be hungry (I just caught on to this), whereas my dad would say, "I'll wait until your mom cooks." Whoa! Feminists, don't start the protest yet. By this time, my dad was a paraplegic, and his scooter didn't fit into the kitchen nor was it safe for him to cook over the stove. I evolved to be a much better cook and people love my food.

I share all of this about my baking history because I was able to connect to those fond memories later as an out-of-control adult. If I didn't love to bake and cook, I doubt I would've had the same success with baking for survival.

I also finally felt like I was in a place to work on the bulimia. I'd be in recovery and then relapse over and over. It took me some time, but bulimia doesn't have a hold on me anymore. I think about engaging or slip up occasionally, but that's just part of the recovery process. For me, if I'm thinking about it or engaging in bulimia, I bring it to therapy. Usually, I'm feeling something is out of control in my life or I'm feeling overwhelmed even if that's not truly the case.

Lessons Learned

- *Recovery starts as soon as you claim it does. Recovery doesn't mean everything is perfect and that you're symptom-free. Also, recovery doesn't end when your symptoms return and/or you relapse. "SAMHSA's working definition of recovery defines recovery as a process of change through which individuals improve their health and wellness, live self-directed lives, and strive to reach their full potential." Visit the Substance Abuse and Mental Health Services Administration for more details visit website.*[6]
- *It's easy to be ashamed of what you lost when you weren't your best. For me, it was sexual indiscretion. I accept this as part of my trauma history and share it to take the power of shame out of it.*
- *What works for your recovery is different than what works for others. For me, baking saved my life. I encourage you to think about ways to cope that are safe so that you can rely on those methods more than the maladaptive ones. I don't have to bake as often anymore, but I know it's there if I need it.*

---

[6] *samhsa.gov/find-help/recovery#:~:text=SAMHSA's%20working%20definition%20of%20recovery,to%20reach%20their%20full%20potential*

ME & MY BESTIE, NATASHA SUBER PERRY (MENDA & TASHA)

Recovery Is Real

Recovery doesn't have an end date. It's an ongoing, everyday process. Recovery does not follow a straight line—it's not linear. It's something you must choose each day to be a part of your life.

Sometimes you'll feel like you've gone backward in your recovery when your mental health slips or relapses. Yet, I choose to believe that you can't go backward in recovery. You learn from the slips, lapses, and full relapses to apply them to your current life. Your learning curve isn't the same as when you first started recovery.

The hits you take along the way can be brutal, but with each new day, you're in a better position to handle life. Each day is an opportunity to carve out or add something new to your recovery.

For me, I do get frustrated that I have to deal with mental health disorders. Due to the type I have, I never know what my tomorrow is going to feel like, although I do know there will be a tomorrow. Some days, I don't participate in recovery and get "stuck" in bed. Some days, recovery is easier than other days and I don't have to think much about doing what's best for my recovery.

I've lost jobs because of my mental health decline. I've had to walk away from opportunities because of the non-linear path of recovery. I've lost friends who couldn't handle my ups and downs. But along the way, I've also gained allies and communities because of my openness in sharing my experiences. I believe I've helped to save and/or improve many lives.

Today, I still fight the good fight to be in recovery. Although it's tough at times, I'm in a much better place than I was before my mental health declined two decades ago. I definitely have the A Squad in clinical support, which isn't the norm in this broken mental health system I have to navigate.

I have a wonderful psychiatrist who has taught me a lot about medication and respects my wishes about which medication side effects are unacceptable to me. I once was taking a medication that interfered with my ability to feel the beat and dance. My psychiatrist, who I've been working with since 2005, understood this wasn't doable.

I'm blessed to be with a therapist I see three times a week. He challenges me, supports me, hurts with me, cheers with me, and always remains in my corner. We've known each other a long time but have worked privately together since 2019—not too long after my dad passed away.

In 2012, I was introduced to the District of Columbia's Department of Behavioral Health's Certified Peer Specialist Program by a case manager when I was doubled over in grief over the loss of my godsister, Scarlet. I decided to apply because I needed something in my life that was just for me. After being accepted, I put in eighty hours of class time plus a field practicum. I learned a lot about mental illness, the system I didn't know I was in, and ways to start advocating for myself and others. My eyes were opened, and I realized the hardest thing in my life that I've had to overcome and continue to overcome is recovery from mental illness.

From there, I knew I needed to learn more about this system and gain credentials to advocate at a higher level. So, I applied and successfully enrolled in a graduate program: Master of Public Health (Health Policy and Management) at George Washington University's Milken Institute School of Public Health. While filling out my application, I didn't hide my mental health recovery. Instead, I highlighted my experiences dealing with the public health system (both to my detriment and success). I would go on to have many successes while undergoing my studies—the biggest of all being selected to be the commencement speaker for the School of Public Health's Matriculation Ceremony. My speech is below. I had invaluable assistance from Robin Delk, the executive coordinator for student and faculty affairs, and Meaghan Wilson, a student advisor at George Washington University's Milken Institute School of Public Health.

Good morning, graduates, faculty, staff, students, family, and friends. Four years ago, when I submitted my application to the School of Public Health, I never dreamed I would be standing here today before a group of my esteemed peers and colleagues, representing our GW community as a speaker.

All of us who have studied public health at GW have been introduced to amazing faculty and staff—and a special network of public health professionals who helped us forge our way through the different components of public health. Being located in the nation's capital created firsthand exposure and opportunities to apply our studies directly in the field, giving us access to leaders of public health.

Public health is our passion. We've studied each other's programs and their application to our own practice. We have learned that public health does not operate in a vacuum and, often, we have to demand a seat at the table. We have learned that, like a well-written novel, public health has many interesting chapters.

We all have stories that highlight areas of public health. Our stories begin where we live, work, and play. I would like to share an excerpt from my public health story, which connects all of our concentrations.

My first chapter begins here in Washington, DC. I am a proud daughter of two native Washingtonians, Deborah and Jeffery Hasbrouck. My father is a Disabled Vietnam-era service-connected veteran, and my mother is his full-time caregiver. My father is a survivor. He survived exposure to a dangerous high-powered radar while in the military. My father was diagnosed with multiple sclerosis and also suffered a spinal cord injury—environmental and occupational health at its worst. Perhaps one of our epidemiology and biostatistics graduates seated here today will lead us closer to finding a cure for multiple sclerosis, cancer, and other debilitating diseases.

Chapter Two begins my personal public health story, and it starts in my second year of law school. While at William and Mary School of Law, my younger brother was injured in a shooting. Soon after, my father's health declined, and he had to be hospitalized. Academics had never been a challenge for me, but for the first time, I couldn't sit for finals. I began a rapid decline into mental illness.

These traumas, paired with earlier traumatic childhood experiences were the catalyst for a decline in my mental health. Fortunately, I asked a dean for help, and she referred me to the counseling center, and I started my entry into the public mental health system which led to the diagnosis of bipolar disorder, PTSD, and bulimia. Although I am far along in my recovery, my journey and resiliency weren't rapid. I had many relapses and hospitalizations. Many public health practitioners helped me along the way, and I became my own advocate for my recovery as I went through the DC public mental health system.

Although most of my treatment has been superb, some experiences caused me additional trauma. During quiet times, I often thought about the struggles of underserved and underrepresented populations. I thought to myself, *I'm educated, I'm strong, I'm resourceful. If harm is coming to me, what's happening to those who can't speak for themselves?* Global health students may closely relate to these health disparity issues.

These specific experiences are unique to me ... but we all play a part in how public health is intertwined into everyone's life.

Chapter Three begins the lifelong recovery process for my dad and me. Because our disabilities require strong medications to help us function, my father and I must incorporate specialized exercise and nutrition-science practices into our daily lives, using exercise, physical activity, and nutrition to keep us healthy. Many governmental systems, practices, and policies—functions of health policy and management—allow for our fullest recovery possible. Genomics research may make it possible for me to treat my mental health disorders with the medication best suited for me genetically. Without the benefits of the Veteran's Administration, the Centers for Medicare and Medicaid Services, and the Social Security Administration, my family's story might be drastically different.

Chapter Four has an interesting twist. I partnered with the DC Department of Behavioral Health and Green Door Behavioral Health to establish Our Door Community Wellness Center, with the mission to promote the evidence that "recovery is real." As executive director, I lead a team that self-identifies about their personal recovery from mental health and/or substance use disorders. We promote prevention and wellness through our community partnerships and services using prevention and community health principles.

In my story, we see how all concentrations played a role in the health concerns within my family. What stories have you been told, witnessed, or lived through?

We came here to better position ourselves as effective advocates in a variety of public health roles. As alumni, we'll continue to grow the connections we've made. We've been given access to the greatest professional network possible while achieving a high standard of educational pursuit.

This has been my public health story. We've all authored our own, and together, our impact will far exceed ourselves as we pave the way for healthier generations. I am public health—and so are you.

I congratulate and commend all of the graduates. If I can take a moment to speak to all in attendance: We, the Class of 2016, thank you for your support. Thank you for the opportunity to **change ourselves—change our communities.** Now, let's go change our world.

Thank you.

May 12, 2016

ME & MOM AKA THE DEBSTER

This One Is for Mom – The Debster

I couldn't write a book and not dedicate a portion to the most important lady in my life, my mommy. Hope you enjoy.

My mother, Deborah Ovena Hasbrouck (née Royal), is an amazing woman. Don't roll your eyes, you'll agree by the end of this passage. If not, we'll have to meet in the parking lot. Just kidding ... kind of—you don't want to meet the Hasbrouck gang in any remote area if we're not happy with how you treat the Debster (my newest nickname for her). There are many ways I could describe my mom (warrior, queen, tiger, goofball, forcefield, etc.). But the Debbie I know (my baby brother Kenneth hates when I call the 'rents by their first name—hey, we have a special relationship) is so much deeper than the visible surface.

If you're privileged enough to really know her, you'll see an adventurous, shy, vulnerable, hesitant, hurt, graceful, prideful woman who's been unfairly designated by her roles instead of her true essence. Many know her as a mother, wife (now widow), daughter, sister, aunt, friend, caregiver, Kenny's mom, Melinda's mom, Tim's mom, etc. They don't see her as just Debbie and sadly nor does she.

My mom thinks her identity is through her family's successes (and failures). She thinks she's living through her children (some of them, let's be real). The mom I've learned about over the years transitioned from this fierce "don't mess with my family" attitude to "I'm just so tired." Before the themes, she had an identity, and now she's gaining it back.

Let me introduce to you Debbie (aka the Debster). Debbie was born in Washington, DC, a younger middle child of many. She was her mom's favorite child (yup, family, I said it—deal) and grew up to be her mom's biggest triumph (my grandmother loved her Debbie). When my grandmother was recovering from surgery or was ill during her last days on Earth, she'd ask for and about my mom. Just hearing me respond was enough for my grandmother's timid smile because I sounded like her. My mom inherited her maternal lineage's legacy of family first. My maternal great-grandmother stepped in front of a bullet meant for someone else—that wasn't family. Imagine the type of person who does that without hesitation, and you'll understand the legacy she (and I) inherited.

There are, of course, tough obligations in this role because you're the thread that sustains the family, and as your thread weakens, so do those who rely on you if they haven't figured out how to weave their own. This legacy will hold you hostage to relationships you desperately want to separate yourself from because they're abusive and/or neglectful. This legacy will destroy your soul if you don't find a way to handle the heaviness of it.

My healing and change have allowed me to positively impact my mom as she seeks ways to courageously unburden her legacy. My mom survived some significant traumas, including temporary foster care; the riots in her high school after the death of Dr. Martin Luther King, Jr.; discrimination from her own race due to the darker color of her beautiful skin; being stationed in isolated locations due to my dad's military service; "best-friends" that turned on her multiple times; jealousy from her church members, friends, and family; ungratefulness on the part of her children (including me); the unfairness by her husband's lack of trying; the death of her baby sister; the tragic death of my dad; and much more. Yet, you won't hear my mom complain about these things.

If you listen and observe closely, you'll see the weight on her shoulders, the desperation in her voice, the fear in her eyes, the pleas for help, and the acceptance of this being life and the lot she faithfully must carry. My mom is all that and a bag of chips because, despite all this and much more, my mom is a goofball. She's a total nut.

Of course, you want examples. I'll oblige. My mom watched Oprah like many people back in the day. One day, I come home from school, and you can tell my mom had been waiting all day to do this. She said, according to Oprah's guest, most wrinkles come from laugh lines. So, to avoid any wrinkles (which my family is notorious for not developing at any age), she was no longer going to smile when she laughed. Yes.

So, for the rest of the day, she laughed without moving her mouth, which only made the observer fall over, laughing hysterically. Go ahead and try it. Now you understand. She used Noxzema at night—

you know, the stuff that gives you a white face on application. She'd regularly plant herself somewhere in the house to wait for an innocent child or my dad to wander by and jump out at them scaring the bleep out of them. Oh, and it didn't matter if you had company over. She'd still do it.

She's tried to unconvincingly prove that she was quite a dancer back in the day. Before going to parties and still to this day, she'd break out in dances, imitating MC Hammer. Her doing the Hammer Dance alone lost cool points but was always so humiliating and hysterical to watch. She picks up random hip-hop culture and will have you dying when she uses it. Once, my brother Tim and I were messing with her and said, "Ma, do the stanky legg!" She was on the porch step and did it perfectly. Bahaaaaaaaaa! Why does she know this move?!

That's my mom, the Debster. Not only do I hope you enjoyed meeting her, but I truly hope you have the pleasure to meet her in person someday.

The End

Shout Outs

There are many people I'd love to thank and acknowledge for helping me get to where I am today.

First, all praise and thanks be to God and to Him alone. For every person helped from my story, all glory goes to God. My purpose is to highlight what He did and does in my life so it may encourage others to hold on and seek a relationship with Him.

I'd like to also thank:

- *My whole family: the Hasbroucks and the Royals.*
- *My immediate family: Dad, Mom, Jeff D., Chawndra (and Michael), Tim, Kenny (and Natascha), and Shayla (and Austin).*

- *My god family: godmother Aunt Beauty, Aunt Lillie, Mr. Earl, Eddie, bestie Tasha, godsister Scarlet, godson Jordan, goddaughter Beauty, and godson Canaan.*
- *My godsister Chris.*
- *Those who've been in my inner circle over the years and held me close to them no matter the circumstances: Tasha, Scarlet, Sowmya, Deena, Johnathan, Jenny, Angie, Cynthia, Monique, Adrienne, Diane, Joya, and Bryan.*
- *The Sista Circle: Angela, Jennifer, Tamara, Malika, Natasha, Shawntae, Stephanie, Elvira, and Denise.*
- *Families that have adopted me: the Suber-Dunn family, the Goings family, the Waters family, and the Pitts-Pickens family.*
- *My Pandemic Bubble: Johhny and Deena—you kept me sane.*
- *My church family and friends at the Temple of Praise,[7] Washington, DC. I'm a member of a great church under the leadership of Bishop Glen A. Staples and Senior Pastor Walter L. Staples. Thank you to everyone who has prayed for me, hugged me, and cried with me.*

---

[7] *thetempleofpraise.org*

- *My clinical support: Dr. R. Kelly Crace, Elise Van Winkle, Katie Blumenthal, Dr. Richard Bebout, Dr. Joel Cohen, Dave Kucharski, Dr. Jami Murray, and Andy Morrow—you each embraced me with warmth, kindness, and greatness. I'm forever grateful.*
- *NAMI DC (National Alliance on Mental Illness, DC Chapter)—one day I walked in and found more than a support group, I found family.*[8]
- *George Washington University, Milken Institute School of Public Health—I went for school and walked away with much more, including two special professors who became mentors: Dr. Olga Price and Dr. Melissa McCarthy.*[9]
- *Black Girl Interrupted Working Group: Mom, Tasha, Johnathan, Bryan, Chawndra, Angie, Cynthia, and Kim—thank you for your faithfulness to me and your unwavering support.*
- *My publishing partner, Global Book Publishing,*[10] *and Founding Partner and CEO Susmita (Sush) Dutta—God blessed me with your presence and passion to take something I've been trying to write for years to completion. My first encounter with you made the 3-hour flight delay invaluable.*

---

[8] *namidc.org*
[9] *publichealth.gwu.edu*
[10] *globalbookpublishing.com*

For those who are no longer present on Earth but are in my life forever, may my book be dedicated to you too: Daddy, Granddad, Grandma, Mom Mae, Iyesha, Aunt Jo-Jo, Aunt Lynn-Lynn, Scarlet, Paul, Jenny, Jackie, and Malika.

Stay up to date and connect with me online at www.bgstories.com.

About the Author

Melinda lives in Washington, DC and self-identifies as a current consumer of mental health services, who is in active recovery from serious mental health disorders, including Bipolar Disorder, Bulimia, Posttraumatic Stress Disorder, and Suicidal Ideation and Attempt. Melinda developed a passion for advocacy, including mental health advocacy from her own experiences healing from her serious mental illnesses utilizing the District of Columbia and Maryland mental/behavioral health system and her law school's counseling center.

Melinda is the Principal Consultant of RoyHas LLC and focuses on transforming systems into human experiences and language. She has a passion for all things public health, including policy, education, and advocacy. Melinda has experience in multiple industry sectors and consults with a variety of stakeholders to help organizations, communities, and individuals evolve above their current circumstances and/or barriers. For more information about RoyHas LLC, please email melinda@royhas.com.

She creatively shares her recovery stories at www.bgstories.com using multiple technology platforms to promote mental health awareness. Melinda shares her unique experiences as a Black woman, an exchange student, traveler, law student, comedian, professor, military brat, researcher, provider, advocate, speaker, and psych patient. Her ease in talking to people from all levels of society, genuine empathy, and personal vulnerability set the stage for deep, real conversations between her and those on her podcast, *Couch Sessions with Melinda Hasbrouck*, due to launch soon.

Melinda currently works as a Program Manager for Amazon, where she has been able to be a public advocate for mental health. She had to take a Leave of Absence due to mental health relapse during 2022 and used her rehabilitation time to complete *Black Girl Interrupted.* Melinda served as a COVID-19 Task Force Division Chief/Program Manager for the DC

Health Department during the start of the Pandemic. She was a Professorial Lecturer at the George Washington University's Milken Institute School of Public Health and guest lectured at the Schools of Medicine and Psychology. Melinda was the founding Executive Director of a new consumer-focused activity center, Our Door Community Wellness Center, a partnership between DC Department of Behavioral Health (DBH) and Green Door Behavioral Health (dissolved). She led the development of the Our Door's programs. Melinda previously worked as a Special Projects Coordinator for DBH's Consumer and Family Affairs Administration.

Melinda received a Master of Public Health (Health Policy and Management) at the George Washington University (GWU) Milken Institute School of Public Health in May 2016 and was the Commencement Speaker for the Public Health graduation ceremony. She received a law degree from William & Mary School of Law in December 2005. Melinda completed her undergraduate studies at Towson University (December 1999).

Melinda dabbles in stand-up comedy, sings really bad karaoke and creatively shares her recovery stories using multiple mediums. She is active throughout the community in various activities that promote mental/behavioral health prevention, recovery, and resiliency. She believes that nonclinical support services in the community are as essential to a person's recovery and resiliency as clinical services. She continues to be an active volunteer, speaker, and advocate for various organizations, including her home church, the Temple of Praise in Washington, DC. She has coordinated and spoken/presented at conferences, local and nationwide, promoting the vision that recovery and resiliency are possible. Melinda was a board member, most recently vice president, of the DC Chapter's National Alliance on Mental Illness (NAMI DC) and has co-facilitated the Wednesday night mixed, support group for individuals with mental illness and those who love them.

@menda76

mhasbrouck

melinda@royhas.com

bgstories.com

Made in the USA
Columbia, SC
11 April 2025

bc7a95f1-c18e-4866-9b0f-deb6b6b7fa17R01